CHRIS KINSLEY

Exploring
BILTMORE ESTATE
from A to Z

THE
History
PRESS

Published by The History Press
Charleston, SC 29403
www.historypress.net

All photographs and photographic elements are courtesy of Wikimedia Commons or an anonymous contributor unless otherwise listed here. All numbered photographs are listed from left to right. Front cover, rabbit courtesy of Matt Reinbold, chick courtesy of Scratchcradle; Page 7, rabbit 1 courtesy of Matt Reinbold, rabbit 2 courtesy of Dakota L.; Page 9, ducks courtesy of Charlesjsharp; Page 11, Conservatory hydrangeas courtesy of Heather Wise; Page 15, frog 1 in water courtesy of Amaila Jonas, frog 2 courtesy of Cornellier; Page 17, chicks 3, 4 and 5 courtesy of Scratchcradle; Page 21, barn interior courtesy of Detlef Scholz; Page 27, koi 1 and 2 courtesy of Tubifex, koi 3 courtesy of Eddie Maloney; Page 29, mouse courtesy of Rasbak; Page 31, fox courtesy of Ken Billington, http://focusingonwildlife.com/news/; Page 33, rhododendrons at Bass Pond courtesy of Vicky Somma; Page 35, owl courtesy of Dick Daniels, http://carolinabirds.org; Page 39, Queen Anne's Lace courtesy of Laurel Wanrow; Page 41, gosling 1 and adult geese courtesy of Jim417, goslings 2, 3 and 4 courtesy of Mike's Birds; Page 43, inchworms courtesy of Judy Gallagher; Page 50, courtesy of Terry Vest; Page 51, tulips courtesy of Ryan White; Page 55, courtesy of The Biltmore Company; Page 56, duck courtesy of nottsexminer; Page 57, courtesy of Brocken Inaglory; Page 63, goats courtesy of The Biltmore Company; Page 65, angel courtesy of Detlef Scholz; Page 66, lilies courtesy of Greenlamplady, koi courtesy of Eddie Maloney; Page 68, Biltmore House rooftop courtesy of Heather Wise; Page 69, gosling courtesy of Mike's Birds; Page 70, sunflowers courtesy of Richard Peña; Page 72, waterfall courtesy of Detlef Scholz; back cover, frog courtesy of Jarek Tuszynski.

First published 2015

Printed in Canada

ISBN 978.1.62619.905.7

Library of Congress Control Number: 2015931731

Notice: The information in this book is true and complete to the best of our knowledge. It is offered without guarantee on the part of the author or The History Press. The author and The History Press disclaim all liability in connection with the use of this book.

For Detlef, because without love,
dreams will never come true.

Many thanks to The Biltmore Company and
J. Banks Smither of The History Press. I'd also
like to thank Karen Grooman and Kim Hardin,
my friends at Biltmore's Gate House Shop, for
believing in this project right from the start. And
to my parents, Hap and Pat Kinsley, thank you for
all your love and support throughout the years.

Biltmore Estate
has so much to see;
let's play "I Spy"
from A to Z!

Aa

Azalea Garden

The morning sun rises
and welcomes the day,

as cottontail bunnies
come out to play.

Bb

Bass Pond

Around the Boat House,
ducklings are gliding,

while down in the thicket,
a heron is hiding.

Cc

Conservatory

A warm sunny room
holds tropical plants,

where flowers are blooming
and butterflies dance.

Dd

Diana

She views the front lawn
from high on the hill,

where two spotted fawns
sleep silent and still.

Ee

Esplanade

Down at the end
of the Esplanade path,

bullfrogs get ready
to jump in the bath.

Ff

Farm

At Antler Hill Farm
where animals stay,

fuzzy chicks hunt
for bugs in the hay.

Gg
Gargoyle

A creature resides
on rooftops and ledges,

where curious spiders
crawl over its edges.

Hh

Horse

A Belgian draft horse
gives rides on the trails,

while barn cats are resting
beside the hay bales.

Ii

Italian Garden

Here is an angel
who quietly spends

his days in the garden
playing with friends.

Jj
Joan of Arc

A statue stands guard
and proudly declares

the strength of her faith
with the cross that she wears.

Kk

Koi

Lily pads float
in elegant pools,

where goldfish and koi
sparkle like jewels.

Ll

Lion

A stone lion sits
   in front of the House,

     providing some shade
      for a brave little mouse.

Mm
Meadow

Over in the meadow
where the grass grows high,

a bashful red fox
sneaks by on the sly.

Nn

Nature

Cool water shimmers
and ripples along,

while bluebirds are filling
the air with their song.

Oo

Observatory

Climb up the stairs
to a room in the sky,

and search for the owl
whooo is perching nearby.

Pp
Pergola

In the Pergola's shade
where wisteria winds,

lizards are racing
across twisted vines.

Qq
Queen Anne's Lace

Ladybugs gather
to check out the scene,

and land on a flower
named after a queen.

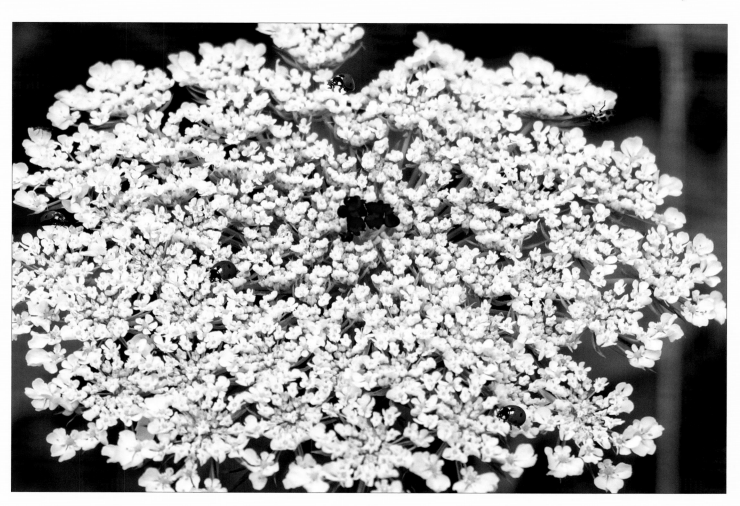

Rr

River

The river rolls by
in the afternoon breeze,

while a family of geese
swims under the trees.

Ss
Sunflowers

Visit this field
and take a quick peek

at tiny inchworms
who play hide-and-seek.

Tt

Tea House

A hungry hawk waits
and watches the ground,

while a snake slithers by,
not making a sound.

Uu

Underground Cellar

In the cool air
of an underground hall,

a camouflaged moth
sleeps on the wall.

Vv

Village

Cedric is waiting
for something to catch,

while Cornelia teaches him
how to play fetch.

Ww

Walled Garden

In a sea of tulips
of purple and pink,

hummingbirds hunt
for nectar to drink.

X x

eXplore

Magical places
are here to discover,

where turtles sunbathe
and dragonflies hover.

Yy
Yuletide Celebrations

A Christmas tree sparkles, festive and bright,

behind a suspended circle of light.

Zz

zzzzzz...

And now you've discovered
what fun it can be

when you explore Biltmore
from A to Z!

Biltmore Estate

ANTLER HILL VILLAGE

F

V

U

S

Q

DEERPARK

CARRIAGE & TRAIL RIDE BARNS

R

Z

H

LAGOON

FRENCH BROAD RIVER

BILTMORE HOUSE

O

G

M

J

L

Y

T

BASS POND

X

N

B

GARDENS

A

C

W

P

K

I

E

D

ANTLER HILL
BARN

WINERY

VILLAGE
HOTEL

INN ON
BILTMORE ESTATE

FRENCH BROAD RIVER

SWANNANOA RIVER

RECEPTION &
TICKETS

ENTRANCE
& EXIT

APPROACH ROAD

MAP NOT TO SCALE

Glossary

Azalea Garden

Established in 1940, the Azalea Garden contains over one thousand azaleas and spans twenty acres, making it Biltmore's largest garden. If guests are lucky enough to see a rabbit here, it will most likely be an eastern cottontail, the most common species in this region. These rabbits run in a zigzag pattern and can reach speeds of up to eighteen miles per hour.

Bass Pond

The Bass Pond was created in 1895 by Frederick Law Olmsted, the landscape architect also known for designing Central Park in New York City. From the rustic Boat House at the Bass Pond, guests can enjoy a view of the pond and perhaps even catch a glimpse of a great blue heron. These large birds hunt for frogs and fish by wading through shallow water and spearing them with their long, sharp bills.

Conservatory

This building's tall, arched windows and glass roof create a warm, sunny environment where plants can be grown year-round. Designed by Biltmore House architect Richard Morris Hunt, it was strategically placed at the bottom of the Walled Garden so that it wouldn't obstruct the view of the Blue Ridge Mountains from the House. Just outside of the Conservatory's front entrance, a terraced Butterfly Garden attracts butterflies each spring with its colorful, sweet-scented flowers.

Diana

Diana, the Roman Goddess of the Hunt, is often portrayed wearing a tunic and carrying an arrow case, or quiver, on her shoulder. Although Diana was known for her hunting skills, she was also known as a protector of woodland animals, including deer. Because Biltmore has a large native deer population, it's not uncommon to come across baby fawns on the property. Although they might appear to have been abandoned, their mothers are likely nearby searching for food.

Esplanade

An esplanade is a long, level, open area for walking. At Biltmore, the Esplanade consists of the expansive front lawn and a limestone structure called the Rampe Douce, which is French for "gentle incline." The Rampe Douce houses a zigzagging staircase that inclines so gradually, even horses are able to ascend its tiny steps without difficulty. At the base of the Rampe Douce, guests will find three sculpted tortoises, distinguished from turtles by their dome-shaped shells and short, sturdy feet.

Farm

The Farm in Antler Hill Village was the center of Biltmore's dairy and farming operations from the early 1900s to the 1950s. The workers and families who lived there formed a close-knit community. Children of these families would ride to their school in Biltmore Village on a "school bus" wagon drawn by two farm horses. Today, guests who visit this area will find farm animals, a renovated barn, old-fashioned tractors and wagons and farm-life demonstrations.

Gargoyle

A gargoyle is a carved stone creature designed to direct water away from a building's roof. Historically, gargoyles were believed to scare away evil spirits. When a gargoyle does not spout water and is used only for decorative purposes, it's called a grotesque. At Biltmore, there are dozens of these hand-carved sculptures on the House and on the buildings in the Stable Courtyard. Look for fantasy creatures resembling angels, elves, dragons, seahorses, monkeys and lions.

Horse

Draft horses are large, muscular horses originally bred to plow fields and haul heavy loads. Weighing up to two thousand pounds, they are known for their strength, patience and gentleness. At Biltmore, guests can find Belgian draft horses at Antler Hill Village and at Deerpark, where they're available to give carriage and trail rides.

Italian Garden

Biltmore's elegant Italian Garden, consisting of three reflecting pools, classical statues and manicured lawns, is its most formal garden. Although this garden was intended as an outdoor "room" for quiet contemplation, its grassy area near the House was once used for recreational activities such as tennis and croquet. Under the stone staircase at the west end of the garden, there's a hidden door. This passageway leads to the basement of the House where the Vanderbilts' guests could change clothes after exercising.

Joan of Arc

Joan of Arc is a fifteenth-century heroine and saint known for inspiring the French army during the Hundred Years' War. This courageous teenage visionary would enter the battlefield sporting the armor and pageboy haircut worn by knights of her era. She is credited with inspiring the bob hairstyle, which was introduced in Paris in 1909 and is still popular today. Guests who look closely at the statue of Joan of Arc on the House's façade will see the cross she wears around her neck.

Koi

The three symmetrical pools in the Italian Garden are filled with brightly colored koi, which are actually domesticated common carp. First bred in China over one thousand years ago, today koi are popular in ornamental water gardens. The word *koi* is Japanese for "carp," and in Japan, these fish are symbols of friendship and love. Along with the colorful koi swimming in the Italian Garden's pools, guests will find goldfish, water snowflakes and Victoria water lilies. These are large lily pads that can grow several feet in diameter, resembling giant cake pans.

Lion

The massive stone lions guarding the entrance of Biltmore House were carved from Italian marble over one hundred years ago. Known for their fierceness, strength and regal grace, lions are symbols of royalty and courage. Dating back to the earliest civilizations, lions have been widely used in palaces, temples and tombs to demonstrate a sense of majesty and awe.

Meadow

The area of open meadows and wooded forests surrounding Biltmore House is known as Deer Park. This 250-acre English-style park is inhabited by wildlife including white-tailed deer, red-tailed hawks, wild turkeys, raccoons, black bears, eastern cottontail rabbits and red foxes. Clever and fast, red foxes have an extraordinary sense of hearing, allowing them to detect the squeaking of a mouse as far as three hundred feet away.

Nature

In this picturesque scene near the arched Bass Pond Bridge, sunshine reflects off the water while birds chirp together in song. Guests strolling along the waterside or relaxing in the shade might even hear the soft, musical call of an eastern bluebird. Biltmore's Bluebird Nest Box Program encourages bluebirds in this area to live and raise families in bluebird boxes placed throughout the estate grounds by volunteers.

Observatory

Biltmore's Observatory is the room at the top of the main entrance tower. George Vanderbilt would take his guests here to admire views of the estate and the surrounding Blue Ridge Mountains. French doors on the Observatory's balcony provide access to the roof, where guests can see gargoyles and architectural features up close. Rooftops and other high perches provide excellent vantage points for great horned owls. When hunting, they scan the ground below for rodents and reptiles, swoop down silently and catch their prey with their sharp, powerful talons.

Pergola

A pergola is a vine-covered garden passageway with columns and a trellis roof. Biltmore's Pergola features stately stone columns, trickling wall fountains and thick vines of bright purple wisteria. Lizards such as eastern fence lizards and five-lined skinks dash around on these vines, looking for insects to eat and basking in the sun.

Queen Anne's Lace

Each summer, this delicate flower graces sunny meadows throughout the estate. According to legend, Queen Anne of England was attempting to sew lace as beautiful as a flower when she pricked her finger. It's said that the tiny red flower in the center of Queen Anne's Lace symbolizes a drop of her blood. Also known as wild carrot, Queen Anne's Lace is harmless, but it should not be confused with poisonous hemlock, which is similar in appearance.

River

The French Broad River is the third oldest river in the world, trailing only the Nile River in Africa and the New River in West Virginia. Although the Cherokee named it Tahkeeostee, meaning "racing waters," the section winding through Biltmore's rolling landscape is usually calm. Canada geese can often be seen here and at the nearby Lagoon, swimming with their families or walking along the banks eating insects and grass.

Sunflowers

Sunflowers at Biltmore bloom in a mile-long field along the French Broad River from July through early September. These bright yellow flowers, which grow up to six feet tall, can contain up to one thousand seeds per flower head. In addition to being beautiful to look at, Biltmore's sunflowers also serve as food for deer, song birds and migrating birds living on the estate.

Tea House

The Tea House was designed by Frederick Law Olmsted, who thought it would be an ideal spot for viewing the expansive mountains to the west. Although the estate originally spanned 125,000 acres, Edith Vanderbilt sold much of it to the federal government in 1915, creating the core of Pisgah National Forest. Today, the estate encompasses 8,000 acres of forestland and is home to birds of prey including red-tailed hawks, bald eagles and great horned owls. Red-tailed hawks have excellent eyesight and can reach speeds of over 120 miles per hour when flying.

Underground Cellar

Guests at Biltmore can walk through the dimly lit stone tunnel lying below the Winery, which was once Biltmore's dairy barn. During the mid-1900s, Biltmore Dairy Farm was a major supplier of milk and ice cream across the South. Always a popular treat at Biltmore, ice cream made appearances at Christmas parties, May Day celebrations, birthday parties and picnics.

Village

In the center of Antler Hill Village is the Village Green, a grassy area where guests enjoy listening to live music and having picnics. Surrounding the Village Green are shops, restaurants, a museum, a hotel and the Winery. In front of Cedric's pub, there's a life-sized bronze statue of Cornelia Vanderbilt playing with the family's beloved Saint Bernard, Cedric. Cornelia holds a ball in her right hand and a magnolia branch in her left, commemorating the magnolia tree planted in the gardens in 1900 to celebrate her birth.

Walled Garden

This four-acre formal garden, consisting of symmetrical flowerbeds and two central arbors, blooms with various flowers from spring through fall. It was originally planned to include fruits and vegetables, but George Vanderbilt requested that it be a decorative garden instead. Each April, seventy-five thousand tulips bloom in the Walled Garden. Hummingbirds, whose favorite color is red, are attracted to the tulips' bright colors. The smallest birds in the world, hummingbirds are also the only birds that can fly in every direction, including upside down and backward.

eXplore

A secluded waterfall is formed where water flows over the Bass Pond's dam into an artfully constructed stone spillway. At the bottom of the waterfall, guests can search for stream life, including turtles, snails, frogs, salamanders and dragonflies. True prehistoric animals, giant dragonflies with wingspans of approximately two and a half feet lived on earth three hundred million years ago, during the late Paleozoic period.

Yuletide Celebrations

On Christmas Eve in 1895, George Vanderbilt opened Biltmore to his family and friends with a festive celebration that's still continued today. During the holiday season, the House is decorated with dozens of Christmas trees, hundreds of wreaths and bows and thousands of ornaments. The Banquet Hall's forty-foot Christmas tree is the largest tree in the House, towering above a chandelier named the "crown of light" by Richard Morris Hunt.

Zzz

The tranquil lake located along the French Broad River is called the Lagoon. This man-made water feature was strategically placed here in order to provide a reflection of the House, which is located on the distant hill above. Guests visiting the Lagoon will find a variety of birds, including mallards, ring-necked ducks and Canada geese. Mallards have the ability to sleep with one eye open, allowing them to be on the alert while they sleep.

Bibliography

ABC News. "Prehistoric-Sized Dragonflies? It's in the Air." http://abcnews.go.com/Technology/DyeHard/story?id=2578773&page=1.

Asheville.com. "Biltmore Installs Bora's Sculpture of 'Cornelia and Cedric.'" http://www.asheville.com/news/biltmore0710b.html.

Ask.com. "What Is the Symbolic Meaning of a Bluebird?" http://www.ask.com/question/what-is-the-symbolic-meaning-of-a-bluebird.

Biltmore.com. "Biltmore's Sunflowers—More Than Just Pretty Faces." http://www.biltmore.com/blog/article/biltmores-sunflowers-more-than-just-pretty-faces.

———. "Insider Tips: Make the Most of Your Summer Visit to Biltmore." http://www.biltmore.com/media/newsarticle/summer-at-biltmore.

———. "Meet Our Staff & Stable." http://www.biltmore.com/more-from-biltmore/equestrian/meet-our-house-and-horses.

Bora Bronze Wheel. "Cornelia and Cedric." http://vadimbora.blogspot.com/2010/08/cornelia-and-cedric.html.

Carley, Rachel, and Rosemary G. Rennicke. *A Pictorial Guide to Biltmore*. Asheville, NC: The Biltmore Company, 2008.

Cohen, Jennie. "Seven Things You Didn't Know about Joan of Arc." http://www.history.com/news/7-things-you-didnt-know-about-joan-of-arc.

Davidson College. "Lizards of North Carolina." http://www.herpsofnc.org/herps_of_NC/lizards/lizards.html.

Dictionary.com. Definition of Pergola. http://dictionary.babylon.com/pergola.

Donnelly, Leeann. "68 Trees in One House? Of Course!" Biltmore.com. http://www.biltmore.com/Blog/article/68-trees-in-one-house-of-course.

Leatherman,Dale Ann, "Chateau in the Carolinas: Visiting Biltmore Estate." Equisearch.com. http://www.equisearch.com/trail_riding/horse_trails/south/eqbiltmore938/2.

McKendree, Sue Clark. "A Technological Tour of the Biltmore Estate." Learn NC. http://www.learnnc.org/lp/editions/biltmore-techtour/1340.

———. "I Scream, You Scream, We All Scream for Ice Cream!" Learn NC. http://www.learnnc.org/lp/pages/1842.

National Geographic. "Cottontail Rabbit." http://animals.nationalgeographic.com/animals/mammals/cottontail-rabbit.

NCWildlife.com. "Leave Fawns and Other Young Wildlife Alone." http://www.ncwildlife.org/Default.aspx?tabid=416&IndexId=9757.

New World Encyclopedia. "Artemis." http://www.newworldencyclopedia.org/entry/Artemis.

O'Sullivan, JoAnne. "Obessessions: Biltmore Dairy Farms." *Carolina Home + Garden* (Spring 2011). http://www.carolinahg.com/Carolina-Home-Garden/Spring-2011/Dairy-King.

Pantas, Lee James. "The Ultimate Guide to Asheville & the Western North Carolina Mountains." AshevilleGuidebook.com.   http://www.ashevilleguidebook.com/wnc/cultural-attractions/biltmore_estate.htm.

———. http://www.ashevilleguidebook.com/wnc/natural-attractions/french_broad_river.htm

Richards, Julie. "How to Dry Sunflower Seeds to Plant." e-How.com. http://www.ehow.com/how_5008880_dry-sunflower-seeds-plant.html.

Ross, Judy. "Winter Birding at Biltmore." Biltmore.com. http://www.biltmore.com/blog/article/winter-birding-at-biltmore.

St. Anne's Church, Kew Green. "Queen Anne's Lace and Damascene Roses." http://www.saintanne-kew.org.uk/forum/celebrate300/epiphany-and-trinity.

We Call It Junkin'. "The Gargoyles of Biltmore Estate." http://www.wecallitjunkin.com/gargoyles-biltmore-estate.

Wikipedia. "Artemis." http://en.wikipedia.org/wiki/Artemis.

———. "Biltmore Estate." http://en.wikipedia.org/wiki/Biltmore_Estate.

———. "Biltmore Farms." http://en.wikipedia.org/wiki/Biltmore_Farms.

———. "Canada Goose." http://en.wikipedia.org/wiki/Canada_Goose.

———. "Cultural Depictions of Lions." http://en.wikipedia.org/wiki/Cultural_depictions_of_lions.

———. "Daucus Carota." http://en.wikipedia.org/wiki/Daucus_carota.

———. "Draft Horse." http://en.wikipedia.org/wiki/Draft_horse.

———. "Eastern Bluebird." http://en.wikipedia.org/wiki/Eastern_Bluebird.

———. "Esplanade." http://en.wikipedia.org/wiki/Esplanade.

———. "Gargoyle." http://en.wikipedia.org/wiki/Gargoyle.

———. "Great Blue Heron." http://en.wikipedia.org/wiki/Great_Blue_Heron.

———. "Great Horned Owl." http://en.wikipedia.org/wiki/Great_Horned_Owl.

———. "Joan of Arc." http://en.wikipedia.org/wiki/Joan_of_arc.

———. "Koi." http://en.wikipedia.org/wiki/Koi.

———. "List of Birds of North Carolina." http://en.wikipedia.org/wiki/List_of_birds_of_North_Carolina.

———. "Red Fox." http://en.wikipedia.org/wiki/Red_fox.

———. "Red-tailed Hawk." http://en.wikipedia.org/wiki/Red_tailed_hawk.

———. "Turtle." http://en.wikipedia.org/wiki/Turtle.

———. "Unihemispheric Slow-wave Sleep." http://en.wikipedia.org/wiki/Unihemispheric_slow-wave_sleep.

———. "Victoria (plant)." http://en.wikipedia.org/wiki/Victoria_Water_Lily.

———. "White Tailed Deer." http://en.wikipedia.org/wiki/White-tailed_deer.

———. "Wildlife of North Carolina." http://en.wikipedia.org/wiki/Wildlife_of_North_Carolina.

Worldofhummingbirds.com. "Hummingbird Facts." http://www.worldofhummingbirds.com/facts.php.

About the Author

Chris Kinsley is a former Biltmore employee and kindergarten teacher who lives in Charlotte, North Carolina. She wrote *Exploring Biltmore Estate from A to Z* to celebrate the beauty of nature found at Biltmore and to provide a fun guidebook for children. Her favorite children's book is *Horton Hatches the Egg* by Dr. Seuss.

Visit us at www.historypress.net